I Am Predestined

Volume 1 of the *I Know Who I Am* Series

I0163336

By Lenita Reeves

Other titles from Lenita Reeves

I Am a Creative, Speaking Spirit

I Am: The Divine Purpose Manifesto

Watchman Responsibility: Winning the End-Time Warfare to Stand Watch and Pray Effectively

How to Teach the Bible with Excellence: Answering the Call to the Teaching Ministry

Fervent Fire: Understanding the Pattern of the Priesthood for Prevailing Intercessory Prayer

The Spirit of Rejection: Heal its Wounds, Restore your Self-Esteem, and Move on to Promotion

Breaking the Silence: The Journey from Rape to Redemption

All available at major online retailers!

Book Description

I Am Predestined
Volume 1 of the *I Know Who I Am* Series

The *I Know Who I Am* series focuses on your identity in Christ and the wonderful, yet often misunderstood, realities of being created in the image and likeness of God. Each volume is a building block for the construction of rightly-focused self-confidence, which is necessary to win in life and take dominion.

If you are unsure of what life holds or tempted to look down on yourself, feel inadequate, or succumb to negative self-talk, this series will give insight into the reality of who you are, and lift your confidence to where it belongs.

Volume 1, *I Am Predestined*, begins by exploring predestination, the first of the three realities the series addresses. In this volume, you discover the rich origins of your life, and truth that transcends mere fate to ascend to the dynamics of destiny. Get ready to be lifted and boldly declare, "I know who I am."

From the Series

I Know Who I Am:
Truths You Need for Confident, Purposeful Living

I Am Predestined
By Lenita Reeves

PurposeHouse Publishing
Copyright © 2018

PurposeHouse
Publishing

Lenita Reeves is founder of the Apostolic and Prophetic Network and author of *Breaking the Silence: The Journey from Rape to Redemption* and more. For more information, visit www.lenitareeves.org.

Dedication

For the body of Christ, the priesthood of believers, that sometimes forgets its own greatness.

Epigraph

I know who I am. – Author

Table of Contents

Acknowledgments

I am grateful for the example of our Lord, Jesus. Even though his own brothers did not believe in him, he continued to believe, and publicly declare, "I am." (John 7:5)

I Am Predestined
By Lenita Reeves

From the *I Know Who I Am* Series

Introduction

Have you ever met someone and secretly admired their confidence? Some people exude confidence—not in a loud or obnoxious way. They are simply firm in their convictions, comfortable in their own skin, and at peace with their strengths as well as their weaknesses. If anyone should exude this quiet strength, shouldn't God's children?

Yet most don't know who God says they are nor the promises at their disposal. They know only that they are saved from hell, that if they die today, they will go to heaven because they have believed and confessed Jesus as Lord. Sadly, they still carry all kinds of issues that affect their confidence for victorious daily living and question the purpose of their lives. Worse still, some are not even convinced of their salvation, and even more do not walk with a resonating reality of who God has made them, where they stand with God, and where they are in their destinies.

The pages of this book have the power to eliminate low living, transform timid mindsets into bold ones, and release greatness hidden underneath the masks of doubt and unbelief. If you are ready for a new reality—a new self-concept—grounded in the truth of the Word, don't stop reading until you've finished the entire series.

It's time for the revelation of kingdom realities that will transform the way you see yourself and how you live your daily life. Get ready to leave your old mindset(s) behind!

Chapter 1: I Am Predestined

Design is a plan for arranging elements in such a way as best to accomplish a particular purpose. – Charles Eames, American Designer

If you've ever embarked on a remodeling project, designed a piece of clothing, or decorated a room, you know that the end result is first conceived in your mind's eye. You may not have had all the details, but there's something you were after. Perhaps your end game was a brighter, sunnier kitchen, an outfit that was just right for a specific occasion, or a design that was as maintenance-free as possible. Whatever the case, you had something in mind.

You live in a world full of design. Whether computers, cars, or clothes, design is all around, and these designs meet a particular need or fulfill a particular function. Employers craft job descriptions because they need a person with a particular skillset to perform a particular function.

They carefully articulate each detail in order to yield the desired result—a qualified candidate.

Designed for an End Game

You may find it easy to think of *things* in terms of design, but Scripture calls *you* a design—a masterpiece, the handiwork of God, and the clay in the potter's hand. God fashion-designed you to yield a particular result—*good works*. And just like any good designer, God had an end game in mind when he designed you. "For I know the thoughts that I think toward you, saith the LORD, thoughts of peace, and not of evil, to give you an *expected end*" (Jeremiah 29:11, KJV, *Emphasis added*).

Do you know your expected end? What is it that you must accomplish on earth in order to hear God say, "Well done, thou good and faithful servant?" Discovering the answer begins with understanding that you have been predestined to good works. God foreordained—preplanned—a certain purpose for you before you were formed in your mother's womb and manifested in the earth.

You see, when it comes to you, God had a particular end in mind before you were even created. There are things that were already laid out for you to know, do, and be before you were even conceived. You were in the mind of God before you were in the womb of a woman.

YOU WERE IN THE MIND OF GOD BEFORE YOU WERE IN THE WOMB OF A WOMAN.

God fashion-designed you to yield a particular result—*good works*.

Your eyes saw my substance, being yet unformed. And in Your book they all were written, The days fashioned for me, When *as yet there were* none of them. (Psalm 139:16 NKJV)

Chapter 2: Predestined for Good Works

God predestined—preplanned— your life and the works you should work on earth. Predestined means:

- to foreordain; determine beforehand
- to decree from eternity (any event, especially the final salvation of individuals) [1]

You did not randomly appear on Earth. You were splendidly designed in the mind of God, and by his very own hand, he crafted you for a particular purpose. According to Ephesians 2:10, you have been *handcrafted* by God.

> For we are His workmanship [His own master work, a work of art], created in Christ Jesus [reborn from above—spiritually transformed, renewed, ready to be used] for good works, which God prepared [for us] beforehand [taking paths which He

---

[1] http://dictionary.reference.com/browse/predestine?s=t

set], so that we would walk in them [living the good life which He prearranged and made ready for us]. (Ephesians 2:10, AMP)

You are his workmanship—his own master design—created in Christ for good works that were prepared for you. There is no other design in the world that is exactly like you because there is no other preordained destiny exactly like yours. You are called to fulfill a particular purpose that was handcrafted—just for you. God laid out your purpose *before* you were born and then designed you to fulfill it.

God articulated this truth to a young prophet, Jeremiah.

Before I formed thee in the belly I knew thee; and before thou camest forth out of the womb I sanctified thee, and I ordained thee a prophet unto the nations. (Jeremiah 1:5, KJV)

The Hebrew meanings of the key words in Jeremiah 1:5, taken from Strong's concordance, follow:

- Formed = to lay out and to squeeze

into shape as a potter, determine or form a resolution in one's mind, fashion, form, frame, maker, potter, purpose
- Belly = hollow of the belly: the womb
- Knew = to ascertain by seeing
- Sanctified = to be clean
- Ordained = to give; to appoint (gave you a prophet's office)

Let's look at this scripture with the Hebrew meanings of the words inserted:

Before I laid you out—just as I laid Adam out on the surface of the ground and formed him from the dust around him—and squeezed you into shape in your mother's womb with the skill of a master potter, I already knew the design I had in mind for you. Like a great designer, I had seen you in my mind's eye and formed a resolution—a manifesto—about your pattern, function, and purpose. Before your mother pushed you out, I had already made you clean and set apart for my purpose and gave you an office for the benefit of nations.

"Well, that was for Jeremiah, not me," you say. "He was a prophet, after all." No, actually, this is for you! According to the New Testament, what was written in the Old Testament is also for your own personal instruction:

> For whatever was written in earlier times was written for our instruction, so that through endurance and the encouragement of the Scriptures we might have hope and overflow with *confidence* in His promises. (Romans 15:4, AMP)

> Now these things happened to them as an example and warning [to us]; they were written for our instruction [to admonish and equip us], upon whom the ends of the ages have come. (1 Corinthians 10:11, AMP)

So God has laid *you* out and squeezed *you* into shape. He had a design in mind for *you*, saw *you* in his mind's eye, and formed a resolution about *your* pattern, function, and purpose. He has made you clean and set apart for his use. You must discover the ministry—*the good works* he has prepared for you as you walk in your gifts and God-given abilities. And whatever ministry he has given you, it is for the benefit of nations, the benefit of others.

It's no wonder that when God began to speak to Abraham about purpose, he spoke to him about a child, for destiny and deliverance were tied to the purpose of the child.

Each child is like an arrow that God has designed to be shot into time and space at a particular moment for a specific purpose. You are also a child of purpose manifested at a particular time and in a particular geographic location as a weapon of God, an arrow, in your land and generation.

EACH CHILD IS LIKE AN ARROW THAT GOD HAS DESIGNED TO BE SHOT INTO TIME AND SPACE AT A PARTICULAR TIME FOR A SPECIFIC PURPOSE.

And hath made of one blood all nations of men for to dwell on all the face of the earth, and hath determined the times before appointed, and the bounds of their habitation. (Acts 17:26, KJV)

Not even the city and state that you were born in is an accident. Everything about you was predestined and planned for a purpose!

Consider the truth spoken by the psalmist, David:

> Thine eyes did see my substance, yet being unperfect; and in thy book all my members were written, which in continuance were fashioned, when as yet there was none of them. (Psalm 139:16, KJV)

> You could see my body grow each passing day. You listed all my parts, and not one of them was missing. (Psalm 139:16, Easy-to-Read Version)

Like a designer, God listed all your parts, wrote all your members in his book, and watched over you as you grew in the womb to ensure his design was accomplished! The world may send you a different message, the challenges of life may beat you down, and someone may have spoken rejection over you out of their own pain—but the truth is you are a masterpiece, God's very own design! God watched over you in the womb! Your life's design was sketched in the book of life in heaven before you came out of the womb. You are precious and predestined—given a predetermined purpose—by God.

> The Lord has made everything for its purpose, even the wicked for the day of trouble. (Proverbs 16:4, English Standard Version (ESV))

Without this understanding, it may be easy to question God or misunderstand or look down upon yourself, thinking, "God, why did you make me this way?" "Why am I not more like my brother or my sister?" "Why am I going through this?" Or, "It would have been better if I would not have been born." The devil is a liar. God made everything for his purpose—that includes you.

God thoughtfully considered everything about you in eternity before you manifested in time. Even the trials you would have to endure were planned.

> This man was handed over to you by God's deliberate plan and foreknowledge; and you, with the help of wicked men, put him to death by nailing him to the cross. (Acts 2:23, New International Version (NIV))

> He was foreknown before the foundation of the world but was made manifest in the last times for the sake of you. (1 Peter 1:20, ESV)

I have two older siblings, and each of us has different personalities, bents, dispositions, passions, gifts, abilities, and skills. Each of us was born at an appointed time and made manifest in time and sequence for a particular reason. We have the same biological father but distinct physical appearances, i.e., skin color, height, and weight. We each experienced our environment and processed the challenges in our family in different ways, and it was all the plan of God. It doesn't take God by surprise because it was his own intelligent design.

The more we understand the *Word of God*, the more we see that DNA is simply man's progress toward understanding God's divine design for each individual, man's attempt at unlocking the divine code that is God's master design called *you*. You must begin to understand these truths about yourself so that as you live, day by day, you are working *with* God's design for you—not against it.

Chapter 3: Daily Appointments with Destiny

Look at this passage of scripture in Psalm 139 and glean another truth from the Word of God:

> Your eyes saw me before I was put together. And all the days of my life were written in your book before any of them came to be. (Psalm 139:16, New Life Version)

> Your eyes saw my substance, being yet unformed. And in Your book they all were written, The days fashioned for me, When as yet there were none of them. (Psalm 139:16, NKJV)

This is why you can truly say that the steps of a righteous man are ordered by the Lord. There is no day or place that you go that takes God by surprise. Each day of your life was laid out and written in God's book before you were born. This is why we have to take daily living very seriously. We have to sort ourselves out on a daily basis, offering up prayers that we would walk in the plan and purposes of God. Have you walked according to purpose, or are you missing your daily appointments with destiny?

HAVE YOU WALKED ACCORDING TO PURPOSE, OR ARE YOU MISSING YOUR DAILY APPOINTMENTS WITH DESTINY?

My sister, my brother, there is something written of you in the volumes of the books of heaven. Your responsibility is to discover and walk it out because, according to Revelation 20:12, you will be held accountable for what is in the books.

> Then said I, Lo, I come: in the volume of the book it is written of me, 8 I delight to do thy will, O my God: yea, thy law is within my heart. (Psalm 40:7-8)

> Then said I, Lo, I come (in the volume of the book it is written of me), to do thy will, O God. (Hebrews 10:7)

> And I saw the dead, small and great,

stand before God; and the books were opened: and another book was opened, which is the book of life: and the dead were judged out of those things which were written in the books, according to their works. (Revelation 20:12)

Realize that what God wrote about you was determined before you were formed in your mother's womb. He predestined you to walk in it. Consider F.B. Meyer's thoughts on Jeremiah 1:5:

From the earliest inception of his being, God had a plan for Jeremiah's career, for which he prepared him. Before the dawn of consciousness, in the very origin of his being, the hands of the great Master Workman reached down out of heaven to shape the plastic clay for the high purpose which he had in view. Note the conjunction of those two expressions: "I appointed and sanctified thee a prophet to the nations;" and again, "I formed thee." God always forms those whom he has appointed and sanctified for any great work.

Ask what thy work in the world is--
that for which thou wast born, to
which thou wast appointed, on
account of which thou wast conceived
in the creative thought of God. That
there is a divine purpose in thy being
is indubitable. Seek that thou mayest
be permitted to realize it. And never
doubt that thou hast been endowed
with all the special aptitudes which
that purpose may demand. God has
formed thee for it, storing thy mind
with all that he knew to be requisite
for thy life-work. It is thy part to
elaborate and improve to the utmost
the two talents which thou hast. Do
not envy another his five. Those three
additional ones were not needed for
the special purpose that thou wast
designed to fulfill.

And it is enough to answer the divine
intention in thy creation,
redemption, or call to service,
whatever it may have been. Do not be
jealous or covetous; it is enough for
thee to be what God made thee to be,
and to be always at thy best. – F. B.

Meyer, Jeremiah Priest and Prophet

The fingerprints of two identical twins are *not* the same.[2] In the same way, God's plan and purpose for you are unique and holy. There are works that he set aside before the foundation of the world for you and you alone to complete. Begin to take the works of God seriously. Begin to understand that there are good works that you have been predestined to work and get busy working the works of God!

> For we are his workmanship, created in Christ Jesus unto good works, which God hath before ordained that we should walk in them. (Ephesians 2:10)

---

[2] University of Cambridge. June 29, 2015. Why are fingerprints unique? Retrieved from http://www.thenakedscientists.com/HTML/questions/question/1000519/

Chapter 4: Predestination: A Spiritual GPS

Don't panic! Predestination means God has already charted out the path of your life from point A to point B to your final destination. He's worked through it all in his mind's eye and he is not surprised by anything you encounter in your daily living. There is a heavenly GPS that has your life's journey pre-programmed. What happens if you miss a turn? The GPS recalculates to make all things work together for your good. The new route may take longer, you may have a different scenic view and new check points; but it will work to make sure you get to your destination.

And we know that all things work together for good to them that love God, to them who are the called according to his purpose. [29] For whom he did foreknow, he also did predestinate to be conformed to the image of his Son, that he might be the firstborn among many brethren.[30] Moreover whom he did predestinate, them he also called: and whom he called, them he also justified: and whom he justified, them he also glorified. (Romans 8:28-30)

Does this mean you and I can sin or do anything we want and still end up at our destination? No. But rather, in all things God works together with those who love him to bring about what is good. It is still the responsibility of the believer to daily present her or himself as a living sacrifice, killing self-will so that the will of God can be manifested.

As you go on your journey, you can be confident that there is a plan in place, and that you don't have to move about aimlessly in life because God has a purpose and predestined works in his plan for you.

Take confidence in the Scripture, which reveals that you have been predestined to:

An Inheritance: Then shall the King say unto them on his right hand, Come, ye blessed of my Father, inherit the kingdom *prepared for you from the foundation of the world.* (Matthew 25:34)

Eternal Life: Now when the Gentiles heard this, they were glad and glorified the word of the Lord. And as many as *had been appointed* to eternal life believed. (Acts 13:48)

A particular geographic location and period of time: And hath made of one blood all nations of men for to dwell on all the face of the earth, and hath *determined the times before appointed*, and the bounds of their habitation. (Acts 17:26)

Be conformed to the image of Jesus: For whom he did foreknow, *he also did predestinate to be conformed to the image of his Son*, that he might be the firstborn among many brethren. (Romans 8:29)

Adoption: *Having predestinated us unto the adoption* of children by Jesus Christ to himself, according to the good pleasure of his will. (Ephesians 1:5)

Purpose: In whom also we have obtained an inheritance, *being predestinated according to the purpose of* *him* who worketh all things after the counsel of his own will. (Ephesians 1:11)

Good works: For we are his workmanship, created in Christ Jesus unto good works, which *God hath before ordained* that we should walk in them. (Ephesians 2:10)

Nothing about you exists by happenstance. God was intentional about your design and finished it beforehand: before you manifested in the earth, he predestined works and purpose for you. Determine to fulfill the counsel and will of God.

BEFORE YOU WERE, I AM HAD A PLAN FOR YOU. BEFORE YOU CAME, HE WROTE PURPOSE PAGES FOR YOU. AS YOU ARE NOW, HE'S PRAYING FOR YOU. AS YOU WILL BE FOREVER, YOU ARE ACCEPTED IN THE BELOVED. —AUTHOR

Walk boldly in the confidence and hope of predestination!

OTHER TITLES

- *I Am: The Divine Purpose Manifesto*
- *I Am a Creative, Speaking Spirit*
- *Watchman Responsibility: Winning the End-Time Warfare to Stand Watch and Pray Effectively*
- *How to Teach the Bible with Excellence: Answering the Call to the Teaching Ministry*
- *Fervent Fire: Understanding the Pattern of the Priesthood for Prevailing Intercessory Prayer*
- *The Spirit of Rejection: Heal its Wounds, Restore your Self-Esteem, and Move on to Promotion*
- *Breaking the Silence: The Journey from Rape to Redemption*
- *Understanding the Power of Agreement: A Necessary Key for Prayer, Relationships, and Progress*
- *Pentecost and the Promise of the Spirit: Understanding the New Covenant, Holy Spirit, and His Gifts*

Now Available from
PurposeHouse Publishing

An Anchor for My Soul:
Soul Stabilizing Devotions for the
Multifaceted, Multi-tasked Woman
by Lenita Reeves

Have you ever asked, "Why do I have to do everything myself?" Today's Christian woman is faced with a dilemma and its name is "multi." While striving to serve the Lord, multiplicities of responsibility vie for her attention. She wrestles to handle it all and at the same time come to grips with her own multifaceted nature. The duty of serving others often overtakes her need for peaceful, quiet times of individual refueling.

An Anchor for My Soul addresses this issue, facilitates "me time," and anchors Christian women who are dizzy and discombobulated from the potter's wheel. Before a ship sets sail, it must be anchored and refueled. This 30-day devotional is the multi-tasked, multifaceted woman's necessary, daily dose of anchoring and refueling.

Connect with Dr. Lenita!

Discover the latest tools and encouragement for living on purpose! Visit (or click) lenitareeves.org and join our mailing list for the latest blog posts and continued news and previews of other upcoming books.

Visit us on social media

Web:
www.lenitareeves.org

Facebook:
http://www.facebook.com/pastorlenita

Instagram:
http://www.instagram.com/pastorlenita

About the Author
Dr. Lenita Reeves

Everyone has fallen but some are in need of the inspiration required to get back up. Through fresh insight delivered in an approachable manner with a twist of real-life humor, Dr. Lenita Reeves inspires audiences to get back up. She is the Founder of PurposeHouse Biblical Counseling, PrayerWatch with Dr. Lenita, and the APT Apostolic and Prophetic Network. Some call her preacher, and some call her teacher, but all agree that she is a prolific voice who speaks with transparency, highlighting her highs as well as her lows to show others that God can turn pain into a platform and use the foolish things of this world to confound the wise.

As a rape survivor and former teen mom, God has graced Lenita to be an outspoken overcomer, sharing her testimony freely and as a result, seeing captives set free all over the world. She is an international speaker and member of the RAINN speaker's bureau. She has traveled as a featured conference speaker in the US, London, Jamaica, Haiti, the Bahamas, Kenya, Uganda, and Ghana, and is the author of several books, all available at http://www.lenitareeves.org/books-by-lenita.

From senior class president to founder of a non-profit, leadership has been an evident mark of Lenita's calling and passions. She has a Bachelor of Science in Industrial Engineering, a Master of Arts in Dance Education, an MBA, and a doctorate in Christian Counseling. She attended Beulah Heights Bible College in Atlanta, Georgia.

A unique blend of education, experiences, and talents positions Lenita to address topics such as: women in leadership, personal leadership discovery, healing from abuse, understanding the purpose of the marriage bed and more. From the brokenhearted to businesspersons to board members, Lenita can relate articulately to their unique challenges.

If you are ready to be inspired by a speaker, if your audience needs to get back up, or just needs a jolt of fresh energy to go to the next level, contact Lenita today. For more information, visit www.lenitareeves.org.